Lindenwood, Fort Wayne Cemetery

Lindenwood Cemetery

Articles of Association, Rules and Regulations Adopted, 1885

Lindenwood, Fort Wayne Cemetery

Lindenwood Cemetery
Articles of Association, Rules and Regulations Adopted, 1885

ISBN/EAN: 9783337159948

Printed in Europe, USA, Canada, Australia, Japan

Cover: Foto ©Andreas Hilbeck / pixelio.de

More available books at **www.hansebooks.com**

List of Officers

OF

LINDENWOOD CEMETERY

(D. G NELSON, President   J. D. BOND, Treasurer

W REITZE, Secretary.

Corporators.

J. L. WILLIAMS,	O. P. MORGAN,	J. H BASS,
H. McCULLOCH,	A P. EDGERTON,	W. H. HOFFMAN
S. B. BOND,	O. A. SIMONS,	J. D. BOND,
I. D. G. NELSON.	GEO. H. WILSON.	A. E. HOFFMAN.

Board of Trustees.

D. G. NELSON,	O. P. MORGAN,	J. L. WILLIAMS,
O A SIMONS		S B. BOND.

JOHN H. DOSWELL,
Superintendent and Landscape Architect.

ARTICLES OF ASSOCIATION

OF THE

LINDENWOOD CEMETERY.

In pursuance of the act of the General Assembly of the State of Indiana, entitled "An act concerning the organization of voluntary associations and repealing former laws in reference thereto, approved February 12, 1855," the undersigned do hereby associate themselves together as a corporation for the objects hereinafter specified:

1st. The corporate name of the corporation shall be "THE LINDENWOOD CEMETERY."

2d. The object of said corporation is to acquire, ornament and dispose of, in suitable lots, land at or near the city of Ft. Wayne, in the county of Allen, in the State of Indiana, for a public Cemetery for the burial of the dead, to be known as the LINDENWOOD CEMETERY at Fort Wayne.

3d. The following described real estate has been purchased by the subscribers hereto for the purposes of said Cemetery, the legal title whereof is now in JESSIE L. WILLIAMS, viz: Situate in the county of Allen, State of Indiana, being that part and portion of section number four (4), in township number thirty (30) north of range number twelve (12) east, which is included within the following metes and bounds, to-wit: Beginning at the southeast corner of said section four (4), thence running west on the south line of said section twenty chains and nine links, thence north seventy-six chains twenty links to the north line of said section, thence east on said north line to the northeast corner of said section nineteen chains ninety-five links, thence south with the east line of said section seventy-six chains twenty links to the place of beginning, containing one hundred fifty-two acres and fifty-five hundredths of an acre, more or less; being lot number one (1) in the subdivision of said section, made by WILLIAM ROCKHILL, SAMUEL EDSALL and JOHN M. WILT, Commissioners appointed in the Allen Circuit Court, at the February term thereof, in the year 1853, to make partition of said section, and to set off to PHILLIP POLLARD in severalty the one-third part in value of said section, and being the same real estate conveyed to said PHILLIP POLLARD on the fifteenth day of September, 1853, by JOSEPH K. EDGERTON, a Commissioner appointed by said Court, by deed bearing that date, and which deed is recorded on pages 204, 205 and 206 in Minute Book Chancery number 2, in Clerk's office of said county of Allen, the date of said record being September 15th, 1853, which real essate, on the completion of the record of these articles, is to be conveyed to said corporation for the purposes thereof.

4th. Until the subscribers hereto are severally paid the amount of their advances for the purchase and improvements of said property, or released from their liability on account thereof, each subscriber shall be deemed an owner or shareholder in said corporation to the amount set opposite his name, and the shares shall be held and be transferable in such manner as the Board of Trustees shall prescribe, and until the Board of Trustees shall otherwise by proper by-laws provide, each subscriber in any election of Trustees or Corporators, or otherwise, shall be entitled to one vote for each twenty-five dollars by him subscribed: *Provided*, however, that when the said subscribers shall be severally reimbursed the amount of their advance, or liabilities for the purchase or improvement of said property, with the interest, or fully released from all such liabilities, all certificates of ownership, of shares or stock in said corporation shall be surrendered and canceled, and the property of said corporation shall thereafter remain and continue a *public trust* in said corporation for the purposes herein expressed.

5th. The subscribers hereto and their successors, corporators of said corporation, shall annually hereafter, or oftener if necessary, fill by election by ballot, from those who may be lot-holders in the Cemetery, all vacancies which may occur among said corporators, and may in like manner increase the number of corporators, so that the number thereof shall never be less than twelve nor more than twenty.

6th. The powers of said corporation shall be vested in a Board of Trustees consisting of five corporators, subscribers hereto, if living and willing and competent to serve, or their successors, chosen as above, to be elected annually by the corporators.

The first Board of Trustees shall be ISAAC D. G. NELSON, JESSE L. WILLIAMS, HUGH McCULLOCH, PLINY HOAGLAND, and DAVID F. COMPARET, who shall hold office for one year, or until their successors are chosen. The Board of Trustees shall elect a President from their own number, and a Secretary and Treasurer, and may from time to time appoint such other officers or agents as may be required to carry out the purposes of said corporation, and may fill any vacancy in the Board of Trustees in the interim between the annual elections, and may make all such by-laws and rules and regulations for the government of said corporation, and the property thereof, and the care, management, and disposal of said cemetery grounds, as may be lawful and proper.

7th. The first annual meeting of corporators for the election of Trustees shall be held at the Clerk's Office of the Allen Circuit Court, in the city of Fort Wayne, on the first Monday of August, A. D. 1860, or such other day as the Board of Trustees may provide, and annually thereafter, at such time and place as the Board of Trustees may from time to time prescribe, who shall also prescribe the rules of election.

8th. So soon after the organization of this corporation as practicable, the Board of Trustees shall provide for laying off for burial purposes so much of the land above described, conveyed to said corporation, as shall be necessary and suitable for such purposes, and if there should be a surplus of said land not required, or not suitable for burial purposes, the same shall be sold in the discretion of said Trustees, and the proceeds thereof, when realized, be applied to the payment of any unpaid purchase money for said land, and to refund to subscribers hereto or their assigns such money as they may have advanced for the purchase of said land, and the improvement of the burial grounds, with the interest thereon, and the residue of such proceeds, if any, be applied in the discretion and under the direction of said Board of Trustees to the beautifying, protecting, and improving said cemetery grounds.

9th. The proceeds of the sale of burial lots, and of any of the land not needed for burial purposes, shall be applied as follows:

First. To the payment to the subscribers hereto, or to their assigns the amount with interest they have already advanced, or may hereafter advance, for the purchase of the land above described, or the improvement of the burial grounds, or to the payment of any obligation or obligations which the corporation may execute for such advances.

Second. To the payment of the purchase money due on said land as it shall become due from the subscribers, or to the payment of any obligation or obligations which the corporation may execute for the amount due on the purchase of said lands.

Third. To enclosing, ornamenting, improving and preserving the Cemetery grounds and defraying necessary expenses, all of which shall be made under the direction and sanction of the Board of Trustees.

10th. The Corporate seal of said Corporation shall be a plain circular seal impressed from a metallic plate or die with the inscription,

"SEAL OF LINDENWOOD CEMETERY."

In witness whereof the undersigned have hereunto interchangeably set their hands at Fort Wayne, this 30th day of July, A. D., 1859:

SUBSCRIBERS' NAMES.	RESIDENCE.	AMOUNT
I. D. G. Nelson	Elm Park	$1,000
Hugh McCulloch	Fort Wayne	1,000
Allen Hamilton	Fort Wayne	1,000
C. D. Bond	Fort Wayne	1,000
J. E. Hill	Fort Wayne	500
A. M. Orbison	Fort Wayne	500
R. W. Taylor	Fort Wayne	1,000
J. L. Williams	Fort Wayne	1,000
A. D. Brandriff	Fort Wayne	1,000
D. F. Comparet	Fort Wayne	1,000
Ochmig Bird	Fort Wayne	1,000
Pliny Hoagland	Fort Wayne	1,000

It will be seen by the foregoing articles of association that the original purpose and aim of the corporators did not originate in any spirit of speculation, such as had been usual in similar organizations, and believed to be the only plan that would enlist sufficient interest and attention to insure success. This report will show elsewhere that the money advanced by the original corporators has been refunded with interest in full, so that they have now only an interest in common with other lot holders. And the reflection that the enterprise has been such a complete success, in all things even far beyond their most sanguine expectations, the corporators feel abundantly compensated for the gratuitous time and attention em-

ployed, as well as for the anxiety felt for the consummation of their desires to see Fort Wayne have a self-supporting, non-speculating cemetery, equal to the best and surpassed by none.

But while indulging in these grateful reflections, it is eminently proper to call to mind the fact that since our organization, one-half of the original corporators, Messrs. Allen Hamilton, Charles D. Bond, John E. Hill, R. W. Taylor, Oehmig Bird and Pliny Hoagland, have gone to their rest, and are now sleeping in the bosom of the earth they took so much interest in purchasing and preparing for the purpose. Of the remaining half, it is not too much to predict, will all follow, long before necessity will require the publication of another report.

Thus, one by one the pioneer workers in this noble, and at first discouraging enterprise, pass away –but Lindenwood Cemetery will *not* pass away until time shall be no more. On the contrary, this beautiful "City of the Dead" will increase in magnitude and interest as each succeeding generation shall enter its portals on their passage to the unknown. Truly may it be said,

> "Though I stoop
> Into a dark, tremendous sea of cloud,
> It is but for a time. I press God's lamp
> Close to my breast ; its splendor soon or late
> Will pierce the gloom. I shall emerge somewhere."

RULES AND REGULATIONS ADOPTED DE-CEMBER, 1885.

- - - ———

CONDITIONS, LIMITATIONS, AND PRIVILEGES TO WHICH EVERY LOT IN LINDENWOOD CEMETERY IS SUBJECT.

I.   The proprietor of any lot or lots shall not have the right to enclose the same with a wall, fence or hedge of any kind. A fence around burial lots, in a well governed cemetery, detracts from the sacredness of the scene, by supposing it possible that such a place would be visited by persons incapable of conducting themselves properly, or that the grounds were pastured with cattle.

II.   No lot or lots shall be used for any other purpose than as a place of burial for the dead, and no trees within the lot or border shall be cut down or destroyed without the consent of the Board of Trustees. This is chiefly to avoid danger to monuments and other improvements on adjoining lots.

III. The proprietor of any lot or lots shall have the right to erect proper stones, monuments, or sepulchral structures (except that no slab shall be set on edge over one foot six inches in height, unless it be at least four inches in thickness), and to cultivate trees, shrubs, and plants in the same. All improvements on lots must be approved of by the Superintendent. All hedges, as well as tender trees and shrubbery, are prohibited by an order passed February 14, 1884.

IV. The proprietor of any lot or lots shall erect at his or her expense, suitable land marks of stone or iron at the corners thereof, and shall also cause the number thereof to be legibly and permanently marked on the premises. And if the proprietor shall fail, for thirty days after notice, to erect such land mark and mark the number thereon, the Board shall have the authority to cause the same to be done at the expense of said proprietor.

V. If the land marks and boundaries of any lot shall be effaced, so that the lot can not with reasonable diligence be identified, the Board shall set off to the said grantee, his or her heirs or assigns, a lot in lieu thereof in such part of the Cemetery as they may see fit, and the lot hereby granted shall, in such case, revert to the corporation.

VI. If any trees or shrubs situated in any lot or lots shall, by means of their roots, branches, or otherwise, become detrimental to the adjacent lots or avenue, or dangerous or inconvenient to passengers, or that may be considered to endanger by falling or otherwise, any monument or other improvement on other lots, it shall be the duty of said Board, and they shall have the right to enter into the said lot and remove the said trees and shrubs, or such parts thereof as are thus detrimental, dangerous, or inconvenient.

VII. If any monument or effigy, or any structure whatever, or any inscription, be placed in or upon any lot which shall be determined by the major part of said Trustees for the time being to be offensive or improper, the said Trustees, or the major part of them, shall have the right, and it shall be their duty, to enter upon said lot and remove the said offensive or improper object or objects.

VIII. The Board of Trustees may from time to time lay out or alter such avenues or walks, and make such rules and regulations for the government of the grounds as they may deem requisite and proper to secure and promote the general objects of the said Cemetery.

IX. The Board informs persons who may wish to obtain lots in this Cemetery that they will have the ground they purchase secured to them and their families and heirs for a burial place *forever*, and for the burial of such other persons as they may choose to admit, provided such admission is free of charge and without any compensation; but owners can not re-sell or transfer their lots to any other person whatever, without the consent of the Board first had and obtained in writing.

X. Lot-holders who may wish to improve their lots, construct vaults or to have their boundaries more fully defined, must apply to the Superintendent, whose directions they will conform to. The Superintendent shall attend all funerals, etc., and it is to him the Board of Trustees look for the enforcement of these rules, and for the maintenance of decorum in the Cemetery on all occasions.

XI. Persons wishing to purchase lots are referred to the office of the Company, or to the Superintendent on the premises, who has the plan of the grounds and every requisite information. No improvement can be commenced on any lot, or interment made therein, until payment therefor has been made or secured in full to the Treasurer.

XII. The Superintendent can not be responsible for not having graves prepared in time for funerals unless he has at least eight hours of daylight previous notice thereof. All orders must be left with the Superintendent of the Cemetery. Suitable grounds have been appropriated for single interments, either for strangers or others.

XIII. In each case of burial, a statement giving the name, nativity, residence, age and cause of death of deceased shall be handed to the Superintendent for registry.

XIV. Persons owning adjoining lots separated by an alley three feet in width may vacate and become the owners of such alley between said lots.

XV. The price to be paid by lot holders to the Superintendent for opening, closing and sodding each adult's grave, shall be $4; for opening, closing and sodding each child's grave, shall be $2.

XVI. For suitable space, opening and closing single graves in what is termed accommodation ground, for strangers and others not owners of lots, $14 for adults and $7 for children will be charged. No disinterment will be allowed without the permission of the Company, lot owner and next of kin of the deceased. The above prices for opening, closing and sodding graves, as well as the prices for burial of strangers are much lower than those of other cemeteries with similar or far less improvements; and not one-half the price of most of them—the object of the Company always having been merely to charge sufficient for this service to defray the current expenses.

XVII. Material for stone or marble work will not be allowed to remain in the Cemetery longer than shall be strictly necessary, and refuse or unused material must be removed as soon as the work is completed. In case of neglect, such removal will be made by the Company at the expense of the lot owner and contractor, who shall be severally responsible. No material of any kind will be received at the Cemetery after 12 o'clock M., on Saturday.

XVIII. The Trustees wish, as far as possible, to discourage the building of vaults, believing, with the best landscape artists of to-day, that they are generally injurious to the appearance of the grounds, and, unless constructed with great care, are apt to leak and are liable to rapid decay, and in course of time to become unsightly ruins. Therefore, except in the section especially set apart for them, no vaults will be permitted to be built, unless the designs for the same are exceptionally good and the construction is solid and thorough. The designs must be submitted to the Trustees and will not be approved unless the structure would, in their judgment, be an architectural ornament to the Cemetery.

XIX. No monument, headstone or coping, and no portion of any vault above ground shall be constructed of other material than cut stone or real bronze. No artificial material will be permitted.

XX. The Board of Trustees shall have the right to make exceptions from the foregoing rules in favor of designs which they consider exceptionally artistic and ornamental, and such exceptions shall not be construed as a rescission of any rules.

XXI. It shall be the right and duty of the Board of Trustees from time to time to lay out and alter such avenues and walks, and to make such rules and regulations for the government of the grounds as they may deem requisite and proper, and calculated to secure and promote the general objects of the Cemetery.

XXII. The Superintendent is directed to enforce the above regulations, and to exclude from the Cemetery any person wilfully violating the same.

REGULATIONS CONCERNING VISITORS.

The Secretary will issue to each proprietor of one or more lots one ticket of admission into the Cemetery under the following regulations, the violation of any of which, or a loan of the ticket, involves a forfeiture of the privilege:

I. No person is to be admitted with a gun, nor are fire-arms of any kind, or fire-crackers, or the like to be discharged on the premises, except such as are appropriate at military funerals.

II. Visitors will be admitted on week days from 9 o'clock A. M. until sundown. All visitors must leave the grounds before dark. On Sundays, admission not until 2 o'clock P. M.

III. No vehicle is to be driven in the Cemetery faster than a walk; and persons are respectfully requested not to drive off of the avenues nor turn on the grass. Drivers must remain on their seats or by their horses during funeral services. All omnibuses, band wagons or similar heavy vehicles are absolutely prohibited.

IV. No horse is to be fastened, except at a post provided for that purpose, and no horse is to be left unfastened without a keeper.

V. All persons are prohibited from gathering flowers, either wild or cultivated, or breaking any tree, shrub, or plant upon the premises.

VI. All persons are prohibited from writing upon, defacing or injuring any monument, fence or other structure in or belonging to the Cemetery.

VII. No money is to be paid by visitors to any person employed upon the Ground.

VIII. Children will not be admitted without their parents or guardians, or some person in charge of them.

IX. No person or party having refreshments of any kind will be permitted to come within the Grounds. Those having baskets or bags of any kind will be required to leave them with the gate-keeper.

X. Except in case of emergency, when lots are required for immediate use, the Superintendent will not attend to the selection or sale of lots on Sunday.

XI. Visitors are reminded that these grounds are sacredly devoted to the interment of the dead, and a strict observance of all that is proper in a place so dedicated will be required of all who visit it.

XII. No visitor will be permitted to disturb the fish, birds or fowls.

The Superintendent and his deputies are invested with full police power to arrest without warrant and take before the Mayor of Fort Wayne or a Justice of the Peace, any offender in these grounds, and the Company exact the discharge of this duty. They will expel from the Cemetery any person disturbing its sanctity by noisy, boisterous or other improper conduct, or who shall violate any of the foregoing rules, and will subject the offender to due punishment.

EARLY HISTORY OF LINDENWOOD CEMETERY.

The necessity of a cemetery for the burial of the dead of the city and vicinity of Fort Wayne, which had been the subject of some solicitude for several years, reached a point at last that fully awakened the citizens to the fact that the only public burial ground of the city, which but a few years previous had been located beyond the limits of the city, was rapidly filling up; and, instead of being a quiet and retired place and a suitable repose for the remains of the dead, was soon destined to be in the midst of the bustle and confusion of business and amusement; and that, too, without an opportunity of extending the grounds to meet the necessities of the future.

The public also became awakened to the alarming fact, that in the original purchase and sale of the grounds for burial purposes, no provision had been made by fixing the price of lots at such rates as would secure a sinking fund, by setting apart a portion of the sales to keep up the grounds after the lots were all sold; or, indeed, any other provision that would secure it from future desecration. It was also seen that the seeds of neglect were already sown and the harvest ripening—decay and destruction had commenced; which began to grieve the hearts of those whose relatives and friends were deposited there. The graves were already being trampled upon by man and beast—monuments and other evidences of departed manhood erected by sorrowing friends, it was evident, were in danger of being defaced and with it their memories perish and be soon forgotten.

The experience of the past was a sufficient warning to the future, that some place should be selected at a suitable distance from the city that would place the danger of its being disturbed by encroachments from its too near proximity to the prospective growth of the city in any contingency, and at the same time of such easy access as to be within the reach of all. Numerous public meetings were held by the citizens and various places suggested. Their location with reference to the roads, crossing of rivers, canals, and rail roads—the ease of access on the one hand, and the impediments on the other—the adaptation of the grounds for the purposes of interment the quality of soil, and all other matters supposed to have a bearing upon the subject, were from time to time discussed, until the most zealous became wearied and discouraged with the prospect of selecting a place that would give general satisfaction.

In this condition matters remained for several months; but the necessity of the case was pressing itself upon the minds of reflecting persons with such intense earnestness, that the different locations, with all the arguments in favor and all the objections urged against them, were canvassed with much freedom and with a *determined will* that a location *must* be made, having as few objections and as many advantages as possible. Fortunately for the public, the minds of several of our citizens soon drifted in the same direction, who secured at the earliest possible moment the grounds now occupied for the purpose; which are so universally admired by the many thousand persons that visit them, amid the wonder and amazement of everybody, how it was that grounds adapted in such a wonderful degree to agricultural purposes should have remained in a state of nature, on the very borders of the city, so long a time; as if by Divine appointment, to be consecrated as the "City of the Dead." Its beautifully diversified surface, with undulating hills, ravines and valleys, fixing, as it were, the very bounds of every section in such an admirable manner as to leave the landscape artist almost at fault to suggest improvements in the execution of his skill. The soil is mostly dry and peculiarly adapted to burial purposes.

On the 5th day of July, 1859, JESSE L. WILLIAMS, HUGH McCULLOCH, CHARLES D. BOND, DAVID F. COMPARET, ROYAL W. TAYLOR, ALLEN HAMILTON, ALEXANDER M. ORBISON, JOHN E. HILL, PLINY HOAGLAND, ALFRED D. BRANDRIFF, OCHMIG BIRD, and ISAAC D. G. NELSON purchased the property set forth in the articles of association, for the sum of $7,627.50, the title for which was to be taken in the name of JESSE L. WILLIAMS for the use of the company, which was duly deeded to the President of Lindenwood Cemetery by the said JESSE L. WILLIAMS, on the 14th day of May, 1860.

The land, when purchased, was in an exceedingly wild condition, nearly the whole ground being covered with timber and a thick growth of underbrush, and what is now the approach, or entrance, an impassable marsh. About sixty-five acres off of the south end of the ground was put under fence, to be occupied for burial and oanamental purposes. All within the enclosure adapted to burial purposes was surveyed into nineteen sections, designated by letter from "A to S" inclusive. Sections B, F and II were laid off into burial lots.

In accordance with the articles of association the Trustees met at their office, in Fort Wayne, on the 14th day of May, 1860, for the purpose of electing the first officers under the organization, which resulted in the election of ISAAC D. G. NELSON as President, and CHARLES D. BOND as Secretary and Treasurer.

The whole expense incurred for improvement at the time of the election, including clearing, fencing, grading, engineering, etc., amounted to $1,841.52, which amount, added to the first payment on the land purchase, made a total of $3,748.39, which sum was advanced by the corporators.

On the 30th day of May, 1860, the grounds were duly set apart for sepulchral purposes with solemn and imposing ceremonies, conducted in the following order:

CONSECRATION OF LINDENWOOD CEMETERY,

WEDNESDAY, MAY 30.

ORDER OF EXERCISES.

1. Reading of the Articles of Association . . . By JESSE L. WILLIAMS.
2. Reading 23d chapter of Genesis . . . . . . By REV. MR. LOWRIE.
3. Dedicatory Prayer . . . . . . By REV. MR. BATTIN.
4. Singing, "I Would not Live Alway" . . . . By THE CHOIR.
5. Reading 39th and 90th Psalms. . . . . . By REV. MR. CURTIS.
6. Dedicatory Poem . . . . By REV. J. M. LOWRIE.
7. Reading 1st Corinthians, 15th chap., com. at 20th v., By REV. MR. RUTHRAUFF.
8. Address . . . . By REV. MR. McMULLEN.
9. Psalm, read . . . . . . By REV. MR. KLINE.
10. Benediction . . . . By REV. MR. ROBINSON.

The weather was beautiful, and everything went off satisfactory. After the exercises were over, the large audience partook of refreshments

provided by themselves, in a social way, on the ground; after which a sale of lots took place, the proceeds of which amounted to about $3,000. In this connection, and as being identified with the early history of this enterprise, it is proper to say that JOHN H. DOSWELL has been Superintendent and Landscape Gardener from the commencement, and to whom the Cemetery is much indebted for the handsome improvements made upon the grounds.

The company is also very greatly indebted to JOHN CHISLET, ESQ., of Pittsburgh, Superintendent and Landscape Gardener of Alleghany Cemetery, for his skill and excellent taste in laying off the grounds originally, and for his many practical suggestions in its management.

To the HON. JOSEPH K. EDGERTON, the stockholders are also under many obligations for the carefully drawn and well digested articles of association, and also for valuable legal advisory information in the original organization.

LAYING OFF THE SECTIONS.

It has been the rule thus far to lay off alternate sections to be occupied for burial purposes, leaving the intermediate sections with most of the timber upon them. This adds somewhat to the expense of keeping up the grounds—but it at the same time so scatters the improvements as to add interest to the diversified scenery in riding or driving along the avenues, and at the same time gives future generations the benefit of lots equal, if not superior, to those now sold. These sections laid off for burial purposes were subdivided into lots of different shapes corresponding with the form and make of the ground, varying in size from 300 square feet to as many thousand, to suit the wants and abilities of different sized families. Single interments and smaller sized lots are also furnished for the use of strangers and others not requiring full sized lots. Ample provision has also been made for the burial of the poor and friendless " without money and without price."

ADAPTABILITY AND FITNESS OF THE GROUND FOR THE PURPOSE.

The selection of grounds for this use away from the busy throng, amid the grove and the forest, is so in keeping with the feelings of our nature to seek seclusion under affliction, that we are involuntarily reminded of the Patriarch Abraham, who, at the death of Sarah, said to the children of Heth, " I am a stranger and sojourner with you ; give me possession of a burial place with you, that I may bury my dead

2

out of my sight. And Abraham came to her tent to mourn and weep for her; and for four hundred shekels of silver he purchased the field of Ephron and the trees that were thereon and the Cave of Macpelah, which was at the end of the field, for a burying place." Jacob also said to his children, "Bury me not in Egypt, but with my fathers in the Cave of Macpelah, that is in the field Ephron. There they buried Abraham and Sarah his wife; there they buried Isaac and Rebecca his wife; and there I buried Leah."

The Egyptians and Persians buried their dead also in large fields and plains surrounded by trees, and the ancient Germans buried their dead in groves consecrated by their Priests. And even the Turks adorn their cemeteries with beautiful avenues, studed with Cypress to shade their walks. So in all ages and in all countries to a greater or less extent, burial locations, decorated with trees, shrubs, plants and flowers, have been made the resting place of the dead. But it is only within a few years that the public mind has been directed to the location and construction of cemeteries in this country, upon a scale appropriate to the fitness of man's destiny and redemption.

The burial ground should not only be the Cemetery for the dead, but also a *Seminary* of learning for the living, when appropriately laid out in suitable lots with walks and carriage roads leading to bold and grand scenery when it can be obtained, and to each dell or more humble shady nook. When such grounds are handsomely embellished and developed by the slight touches of the hand of art, and planted with trees, shrubs, vines, etc., many, perhaps for the first time, will be moved with higher emotions and loftier conceptions of the Author of their being.

But not so with visits made to the deserted and neglected grave yard as we hasten away after depositing the remains of some relative or friend, as if anxious to forget the spot and the sad scene, never to return, except to experience similar sensations, heightened by the contemplation that our own bodies must soon be treated with the same indifference and neglect.

Let us then make our own "Lindenwood" pleasant and attractive, where we may often go, with a pleasure not easily described, to contemplate the scenes of future bliss that await those sleeping around us. Here, under the shades of these stately monarchs of the forest, we can look out upon nature's wild wood, the grassy lawn dotted here and there with groups of evergreens, interspersed with roses and flowers, to soften the heart and charm the soul—a secluded, cultivated scene, awaking no thoughts of pretension and display—but rather of simplicity, quiet security, affectionate remembrance, cheerful hope.

A Glance at the Future as Set Forth in Our First Report.

Notwithstanding the amount of improvements already made, the good work has scarcely begun. The graveling of the avenues and walks is a tedious and expensive job, but will be prosecuted where most needed as fast as is practicable. Considerable filling up has to be done, timber removed off some of the sections, etc. It is also the purpose of the Association to excavate two Lakes, which can be done without heavy expense, and when completed will add immensely to the beauty of the scenery, which nature has so lavishly bestowed upon these grounds.

The completion of all these and others not enumerated, in addition to the regular business of the Cemetery, will cost a large sum of money. It cannot be done at once, yet we have the assurance that it *will* be done —and most of it at no very distant day. The enterprise is no longer an experiment. It has been successful beyond the expectation of its most sanguine friends; and, although the present liability of the Company amounts to about eight thousand dollars, all of which has to be paid within three years, besides refunding the stockholders if they require it; still those who witnessed the dark hours of its early history and combated an opposition more of indifference than open opjection—the alarms of war that suddenly broke upon the country—a heavy debt and rapidly accumulating expenses, all conspiring to shake the confidence of the Company and produce discouragement, certainly will see no cause for discouragement now. As they never faltered then, but with a fixed determination pressed on the work and met every assessment for funds that was made upon them with a promptness and determination of purpose that so generally accomplishes success, so they will see now that this good work goes on.

In brief, it is the purpose of those having this enterprise in charge to use all the means, after the payment of expenses, in beautifying these grounds that are to be made the last resting place of us all, trusting that those who follow them will emulate the example and will go on increasing the interest from generation to generation, until the humble spot now so dear to some of us, because of the incidents and events of early associations, began as it was in the midst of a forest, under gloomy and discouraging auspices, will become one day one of the most attractive places of rural interest in Northern Indiana. No change in its objects or purposes can ever be made; but it will ever remain as it was consecrated, without "let or hindrance," "The City of the Dead." Here in these groves, which were God's first temples, the dead are to be "buried out of our sight," in the virgin soil that was never cultivated by man. It will be the " Beautiful City," peopled with its thousands of voiceless tenants, and visited by its tens of thousands of living beings, to witness the storied urn, the " animated bust," the noble obelisk, the mausoleum, the richly sculptured tomb, and the more plain and humble slab, telling the brief story of a thousand lives. Here, also, will Flora gem the ground with her jewels, and perfume the air with her incense. Here the cedar, the fir, the spruce, the box, the pine and the arborvitæ, with other evergreens from many climes, emblems of immortality, and historical trees will mingle their shadows together. Here the cypress and the laurel will interlace their branches. Here, too, the mighty oaks, with their giant outstretched arms, that have bid defiance to the frosts and tempests of a thousand winters, will still remain for generations as monuments of passing ages. Here, too, will be preserved and cultivated, with a view to the expanding of their wildest beauties, all the other varieties of trees and shrubs, to add to the many other charms that will ever grace these grounds. " May they never be marred by mistaken taste or desecrated by rude hands, but beneath the green and waving foliage—amid tranquil shades where nature weeps in all her dews, and sighs in every breeze, and chants a requiem by each warbling bird—the dying generations of this growing city and surrounding country will henceforth be sepulchered."

NOTE. In how far the above predictions have been verified this report will show elsewhere.

THE GROUNDS OPEN TO EVERYBODY.

As we pass on, we wish to drop a word to our country friends. It is not necessary for us to say to them that they are invited to bury in these grounds. The articles of association explain the object and purposes of the organization, which are, that all who choose to do so may here find a resting place for themselves and friends ; but it is to direct their attention to the fact that this is the only safe place of burial, within many miles at least, where they can be assured that their ashes can remain undisturbed until the resurrection morn. Burials upon their own private grounds, because they own the farm, is the worst of all. How long they or their descendants will remain the owners they know not. Sad scenes enough have come under the eyes of us all, that should cause the mind to revolt

EDGERTON

at thoughts of such a burial. But even all the best regulated country grave-yards become sooner or later filled; friends become scattered; generations pass away; grave-yards, first neglected, then deserted, and memories allowed to perish amid the silent sighs of departed humanity. This is the history of older sections of this country, and of the world.

We, therefore, wish simply to direct all within reasonable distance to contemplate these facts, and have them feel that the portals of " Lindenwood " are open to all who wish to enter.

And this suggests another advantage over rural cemeteries—their influence on the moral feelings. Can any good come from visiting old-fashioned grave-yards, barbarously kept as many of them are? Who has not been shocked at seeing their rude hillocks, crowded together in dreary rows, perhaps grassless, or covered with rank weeds and briars, their head-stones tilted over at all angles, or broken and prostrate? Was any one ever made better by walking through a burying-ground used as a sheep pasture, or left open to the street by a broken fence, or allowed to stand treeless and shrubless, exposed to the glaring sun and howling wind? Such sights sadden us, indeed; but they do not mend our hearts. They remind us that we must die; but they also make us dread to die—dread to think that our bodies must be put into the same festering earth, and be treated with the same neglect.

But why clothe death with such unnecessary terrors? It is sad enough to turn away from life and all we hold dear, without adding to the sadness by rendering the grave an object of disgust and dismay. Rather, let us make our burial-grounds pleasant and attractive; places where we shall be inclined to go often, to muse upon life and its grandest concerns, and upon death and the glorious rewards awaiting the good after death, to reflect upon the virtues of those whose dust sleeps around us, and to consider how we may imitate those virtues. The spirit of Themistocles was fired by visiting the tombs of the illustrious dead. "The Romans buried their most honored citizens along the Appian Way, that the youth as they entered the city might be moved to emulate their virtues and share their renown." The early Christians worshiped near the graves of the martyrs, that they might be filled with their spirit. And so, may not we, while walking among the tombs of the good departed, catch something of their spirit and be filled with aspirations after a better life?

There should be nothing in the place or manner of their interment to detract from our tender and respectful veneration for the dead. But this can hardly be avoided, if their graves are dug in a dismal and unsightly spot. How much better to choose some retired, sunny slope, the most beautiful in the region around us, and make it sacred as a burial place forever. Here let there be trees with their grateful and soul-absorbing shade; there let us see the open lawn and cheerful sunshine; around us, on every hand, let us behold the opening bud and springing seed, types of the resurrection.

———

THE OLD BROADWAY CEMETERY.

The following letter from the Hon. Hugh McCulloch was received in answer to certain inquiries made for the purpose of obtaining some unwritten historical facts in regard to the origin of the old Broadway Cemetery, as well as the disposition he contemplated making of the property, as it is no longer a sacred burying place for the dead, but has become an unsightly abomination to the living. The letter explains itself, containing a praiseworthy offer from Mr. McCulloch to donate the ground to the city for the purposes of a public park, upon condition that it shall forever be kept up as such.

It would be a small park, to be sure, but, if nothing more, it would serve as a breathing place, at least, for those who are so confined in their narrow apartments that they have not at present even that much of God's fresh air to enjoy. Anything of the kind, however small, will afford some of the pleasures and comforts now denied to all classes and conditions of our people. Its location is so admirable for convenience that all can visit it at pleasure:

P. O. Box 646—WASHINGTON, D. C., {
November 24, '85. {

DEAR SIR—Yours of the 18th inst. is at hand. Soon after I became a resident of Fort Wayne, I discovered that there was, neither in the town nor near it, a public burial ground. That the interments had been and were being made in a lot to which the town had no title, and that consequently there could be no assurance that the bodies buried there would remain undisturbed, I, therefore, in 1837, if I rightly recollect, bought of Judge Hanna four acres of land near the town, enclosed them with a handsome fence, and laid them off into burial lots. A part of the lots were set apart for the poor, the rest were offered for sale and a part of them, perhaps the larger part, were sold before the Lindenwood Cemetery Company was formed. The proceeds of the sales were applied to the payment of the money I had expended in the purchase and improvement of the ground. For my trouble I expected and received no compensation. The sale of the lots ceased soon after the Lindenwood Cemetery was established, and as there were no funds for keeping the ground in order, and as a large part of the bodies which had been buried there were removed to the new cemetery, they were neglected and are now, I understand, in a disreputable condition. As the lots were sold for burial purposes only, the property reverts to me when it ceases to be used for burial purposes. Under these circumstances, I have offered to relinquish my right to it to the City of Fort Wayne, upon an agreement of the city to properly enclose and beautify it, and permanently maintain it as a "Public Park." I am, very truly yours,

HUGH McCULLOCH.

I. D. G. NELSON, Esq.

REAL ESTATE TRANSACTIONS.

ORIGINAL PURCHASES, QUANTITIES, PRICES—OF WHOM PURCHASED
AND TO WHOM SOLD.

Sept. 29, 1859.	Of Jesse L. Williams, 152 55-100 acres . .	$7,627 50
Jan. 2, 1864.	Of Geo. W. and A. W. Ewing, 21 acres .	1,850 00
Sept. 6, 1864.	Of William G. Ewing, Jr., 7 acres. . . .	630 00
Jan. 25, 1882.	Of N. Y. C. and St. Louis Railway strip of land along canal of indefinite quantity, described below. There was no money consideration, but a mutual exchange of privileges.	

PROPERTY SOLD NOT SUITED TO BURIAL PURPOSES.

Sept. 18, 1864.	To Susan B. Beierlein, 6 44-100 acres across canal	$500 00
Nov. 24, 1881.	To John H. Bass, 42½ acres across railway .	3,825 00
Jan. 2, 1882.	To N. Y. C. & St. L. Ry., 3 16-100 acres right of way	205 40

In addition to the above statement, a sale of a regularly laid off section ("Y"), lying on the west border of the grounds, containing about two acres, was sold March 17, 1884, to the "Achduth Veshalom Congregation" for the sum of three thousand dollars for the purposes of Hebrew burial. This embraces all the outside sales made of any description. What other sales have been made has been in lots for burial purposes on regularly laid off sections—a list of which is published elsewhere. The section sold to the Hebrews, although for their own use and purposes, is subject to the same rules and regulations as govern other portions of the Cemetery.

MAP OF THE GROUND.

A fine lithographed map, copied from a careful survey made and platted by Superintendent Doswell, is herewith submitted, which shows accurately the entire property as now owned by Lindenwood Cemetery Corporation, with the sections as laid off and designated by letters, avenues, etc. The survey shows that there are 124 acres of ground after making all deductions, 70 acres of which are suitable for interments, a small portion of which only has been thus far used. It has been found to be bad economy for cemetery companies to hold much more real estate than is needed for reasonable use ; contrary to a practice once considered necessary—experience having demonstrated that no difficulty is ever found in purchasing suitable ground for interments adjoining a cemetery at reasonable prices—so that upon every consideration of utility, necessity and economy sufficient, at most for a generation, is ample for any cemetery to own. That much it will be seen we have, and much more, according to the ratio of interments heretofore made.

NEW ENTRANCE TO THE GROUNDS AS SHOWN BY THE FRONTISPIECE TO THIS REPORT.

Lindenwood Cemetery has now as attractive, pleasing and convenient an approach to the main grounds for funeral processions, or for accomodation of visitors, as any cemetery in the country. But it was the work of years to accomplish it. It is only those immediately connected with the enterprise, who can ever understand the perplexities anxieties and troubles for the want of it, or in endeavoring to remove obstacles that existed at the time the ground was purchased—the removal of which was from the first and at the time of purchase considered indispensable, as will be seen by reference to our first report. After fruitless efforts for a quarter of a century to no purpose, and almost reaching at last to the verge of despondency in endeavoring to secure what we wanted and so much needed, Providence at last seemed to interpose and made it possible.

There was but one apparently natural, commanding entrance point to the grounds, and that led over a canal culvert too small to pass the

water in time of heavy rains, overflowing the passage way to the great annoyance of funeral processions, through slough holes and other water obstructions, all lying at the very entrance gate, reputed to be owned by foreign canal bond holders or other complicated titles. Although it was of no actual value to the property holders, still a conveyance seemed difficult, if not impossible, to obtain. Besides this, a much traveled circuitous public road existing and used for over forty years, passed along and ran immediately up to where our entrance gate should properly be, and where it is now placed. At last the long hoped for time arrived for a change in the line of the road, for the purpose of making it a free gravel pike. The County Commissioners ordered a survey and re-location where crooked or necessary, and appointed viewers for the purpose, who with extraordinary good sense changed the curve of the old road to a better route, and on a straight line where it naturally should be for the convenience of the cemetery and for the accommodation of the traveling public as well. At about this juncture the N. Y., St. L. & C. R'y purchased the Wabash & Erie Canal interest for a road bed—this included the property at our entrance that we had so long wanted. Their survey for location of the road took them over a piece of our cemetery grounds on the north. According to our statutes protecting cemetery grounds from being taken for public use, they were estopped altogether, unless with our consent; which the Trustees agreed to upon condition of payment as in other cases, and by WM. B. HOWARD, the representive man, deeding to the cemetery the strip of land required to complete our front entrance as described elsewhere, which was accordingly agreed to, and the work of filling, leveling and grading the ground at once commenced, preparatory to a general improvement by the construction of a superb iron fence 1,700 feet in length, extending along the east front and along the entire distance of the south line of the cemetery and public highway. The fence is five feet high, set upon stone posts 8x8, three feet in the ground. It was constructed by Messrs. Seward & Co., of Bloomington, Indiana, at a cost of $2,652.25, and will last for generations.

A plan for a lodge with bell tower, office, etc., was also proposed, and Messrs. Wing & Mahurin instructed to furnish a plan, which with some modifications was adopted as follows, and built on contract by Messrs. Wm. & J. J. Geake, at a cost of $6,961.29. It is a beautiful and attractive structure.

DESCRIPTION OF BUILDING.

The "Gate Lodge," built in that *picturesque* style of Gothic architecture, not romantic in its expressions, but impressive to a solemn degree, is located just inside the entrance gates, covering a space thirty-five feet by thirty-one feet, and contains a private office for the Board of Trustees, a reception or waiting-room for the public, and ladies' and gentlemen's private retiring-rooms, the floors of which are laid with black and white marble tile, and the various rooms wainscoted with marbleized slate in imitation of red Scotch and green serpentine granite, while the walls and grained ceilings are neatly frescoed in a tasteful manner. The base of the building is of Bedford, Ind., Oolitic lime-stone, and above this, to the gutters, of Stony Point, Michigan, sand-stone—soft *quarrie* or rock face. A circular bell-tower breaks out in one of the angles, and at the base is an open loggia leading to both the private office and reception-room. A steep pitched roof, covered with dark and ornamental slate, with terra cotta cresting and finials, the whole forming a graceful mass, and assuming a solemn and dignified appearance, which, on the first approach of all who visit "Lindenwood," it bespeaks the hallowed grandeur of the final resting place of the relatives and friends sleeping the eternal sleep beyond its walls.

THE HEBREW SECTION.

On the 17th day of March, 1884, the Trustees sold and deeded section "Y," containing about three acres, lying on the west border of the Cemetery grounds, to the "Achduth Veshalom Congregation," for their exclusive use for burial purposes, but to be governed by the same general rules and regulations as those adopted by the Trustees in other cases. This section is handsomely located, having a commanding view of the "Twin Lakes" and other improved portions of the grounds. The well-known characteristics of this class of our citizens is an assurance that after they complete the removal of their dead from their old burial grounds, they will fit up their new, beautiful, natural location in such tasteful manner as will make it as attractive as other and older portions of Lindenwood.

THE LAKES IN LINDENWOOD,

Two in number, or rather three as they are constructed and appear on the plat of the ground, are of unassuming proportions, but sufficient for the extent of the other improvements. The plat attached, as well as the lithographed view of the entrance, shows the location of Glen Lake as we enter the grounds, passing it as we drive along the avenue toward Glen Circle, at the junction of sections F, G and J, so named because of the peculiar characteristics of ground and surroundings, by John Chislett, Esq., the surveyor and landscape gardener of Pittsburg, Pa., who laid off the sections and located the avenues just as nature had provided, as he expressed it, leaving very little for him to do—adding this in his report to the Trustees after his work was completed:

"Your ground is so admirably suited for the purpose that at first sight I was quite charmed to find a spot so varied and picturesque in your otherwise level country, and one combining so many qualities to render it a beautiful "rural cemetery." Upon a closer examination I found all these qualities true to their appearance. The soil is light, porous and sandy, and of that anti-septic nature so much desired by many. The effect of water in landscape scenery should not be overlooked. Whether it be in the running brook or spread out in the form of a miniature lake, it always adds a charm to every scene, refreshes an open view, and animates a shade. In this respect you have a resource for producing some of the finest effects—

"'The rivulet spread
Into a liquid plain there stood unmoved,
Reflecting the expanse of Heaven above.'"

Returning to the subject of Glen Lake, it is proper to say that it is supplied with water from never-failing springs and other sources that sometimes heretofore have given us more than we need, and to our injury; but the excess is now permanently provided for by the construction of a substantial culvert of ample capacity. A small natural island with a still smaller rustic house upon it, for the shelter of the Superintendent's water fowls, which is mostly hidden by small trees and underbrush in their wild state, giving the whole a picturesque and romantic appearance. The lake is stocked with German carp, which are doing nicely.

Besides this lake on the east border of the grounds, there are on the west side of the grounds, immediately fronting and skirting the border of Section II, there lies, nestling in the lap of nature, where the setting sun smiles sweetly on the waters of the "Twin Sisters," two lakes in one, separated by a narrow *strait*, or passage of water from one to the other, in its circuitous route to the river, which, when there is an excess of water, flows over a protected waste-way constructed for the purpose of preventing the resident fish from floating out of the lake, as well as to prevent the bass and other flesh-eating fish from running up and over into the lake during high water, and feasting upon the non-combative carp, with which these waters have also recently been stocked.

These lakes can be readily enlarged cheaply by adding an area of several acres, which will doutless be done at no distant day. The surface soil taken out in excavating for that purpose is, for several inches in depth, composed of a deep, rich, vegetable mould, which can be profitably utilized as a top dressing on lots that need fertilizing.

At the separation of the two lakes here referred to, a small rustic bridge spans the strait, as a crossing for the new attractive avenue that stretches up the gentle rise to the Hebrew section, Y, making an interesting and pleasing drive for those wishing to visit and observe all the beauties of Lindenwood.

Graveyard Neglect and Desecration.

The following sad commentary upon the condition of Greenlawn Cemetery in Indianapolis, published in the *Herald*, having such a peculiar application to our own Broadway Cemetery (except that theirs is yet enclosed, while ours is an open waste), that we publish it for the deep and sad, yet beautiful, thoughts it contains:

"Greenlawn Cemetery is a neglected garden of the dead. Separated from the busy city which surrounds it by a rude board fence, high straight and grim, it is a gloomy forest of broken grave-stones, ruined vaults, dying sycamores and tangled vines. Steaming engines shriek around it; the roar and rattle of the streets pervade it; the noise of hundreds of whirling wheels of manufactories re-echo through it; and the smoke from the towering chimneys covers it like a pall. Within its gates is the gloom of desolation. The grass grows year after year, and dies uncut. The rank weeds that neglect cultivates flourish defiantly over the buried forms of its many sleepers. Green ivies mingle their glossy leaves with the autumn-tinted woodbine and the purple berries of the deadly nightshade. All day long the sparrows twitter and chirp in the sweet security of its neglected trees. The ground-squirrels chatter saucily at each other, and courageously wander over the unkempt ground. The spiders weave their webs unmolested in the tangled bushes; the bees hum about the few flowers that dare to rear their heads above the rank decay; and the voices of myriads of insects continually murmur their sad refrain. Decay has touched this field of graves with his withering hand, and its beauties change to ruins. The graves which once were banked high, covered with flowers, and marked by imposing monuments, are now sunken, the flowers smothered in poisonous weeds, the monuments shattered and in ruins.

"As the years went by, and Greenlawn was fast becoming condemned ground, many removed their dead to Crown Hill. Hundreds who sleep the dreamless sleep in Greenlawn are no longer held in sweet remembrance by any living being. All that were dear to them have, like them, gone the dim way of destiny, through the shadowy gates of death. We stand by their neglected graves and wonder at the mysteries which were before them, and are about them, and are around us all. We remember that once they were 'moving shadows' on the stage of existence, like ourselves. The infinite egoism of the soul was as strong within them. They lived, and loved, and toiled, and suffered. They died; and all our knowledge and

SIMONS

longing can pursue them no farther. In all the silent city there is no voice to tell us the secret of death. We can think of their brief lives, and see them, as they once were, ahead of us in the grand procession to the grave; but we cannot wring from their mouldering lips one word of infinite knowledge.

> "'They loved; but the story we cannot unfold;
> They scorned; but the heart of the haughty is cold;
> They grieved; but no wail from their slumbers will come;
> They joyed; but the tongue of their gladness is dumb."

LINDENWOOD CEMETERY—NOT A PARK.

The following inquiry was once made by a newspaper correspondent: "What is Fort Wayne doing in the way of a park? It is hardly fair to call Lindenwood Cemetery a park; and yet it is the only thing of the kind about Fort Wayne." The correspondent still referring to the cemetery, makes the following significant inquiry: "Why should it be made a place of public resort for the promiscuous and common use of the citizens of the city at large?" And then adds: "It is said that the city has never yet contributed a dollar in any manner towards it; but perhaps it has never been asked to do so. It is, however, quite certain that a very large amount of money and skill has been expended there, which makes it the feature of attraction about the city. Strangers visiting the city who have seen it are at once captivated by its many attractions, notwithstanding it is but the city of the dead. It is not properly a park, and should not be so considered."

With reference to the above it is eminently proper to say that there has never been a city, county or township contribution towards the purchase of the grounds, or in payment of any of the improvements. Hence it is strictly a cemetery for the burial of the dead, owned exclusively by the Lindenwood corporation, and should be regarded and treated as such by all visitors, and not as a pleasure-ground for everybody to congregate at any and all times for purposes of amusement, as if it were in fact a public park, for joyous and hilarious meetings at their convenience.

In the absence of any place for recreation and mutual enjoyment, this has been tolerated heretofore to the extreme limit of propriety, and must be discontinued. Fort Wayne can afford it, and ought to have, one or more public parks, free and open to any and all of its citizens. It is one of the great needs of the city, which ought to be promptly provided for—a sentiment that surely will meet with a ready response from every good citizen and thoughtful person.

In referring to Lindenwood Cemetery, it must be kept in remembrance that it is not merely a place for the burial of the dead "out of our sight," as some would have it.   Although it is but a quarter of a century ago that it was a wild and unsightly forest, covered with heavy timber and an astonishing growth of underbrush, with occasional wet and marshy places and unsightly swales, yet it has nevertheless all been reclaimed and beautified by converting its swales and marshes into beautiful lakes, meadows and lawns, and the rolling upland into appropriate sections of various sizes for sepulchral purposes and for ornamentation, and the whole beautifully carpeted with nature's richest green velvety covering.

This reclaimed ground, that has been made so beautiful by artistic hands, was duly consecrated to the solemn use of a common sepulture, where sorrowing friends are expected to visit the graves of departed relatives and friends for quiet meditation, at such times as may be convenient, undisturbed by hilarious crowds of thoughtless visitors.   When properly considered the rural cemetery, such as Lindenwood is, should be regarded as a school for meditation and thought, to cultivate the mind in the presence of the beauties of nature combined with art, as seen in the surroundings, that may teach some of us in our thoughtful moments, as we look upon the green covering with which nature has covered the grave in which lies the dearest treasure of the heart, we will unconsciously ask ourselves the question, "Shall we meet again?"   Then the response will come, as we stand beneath the giant oak, the monarch of the forest stretching up toward heaven, or the evergreen trees, symbols of immortality, around us; and the arched mound at our feet, that is kept green and fragrant with the tears of affection, "Yes, we shall meet again." Thus new hopes and aspirations enter into the crushed heart, and the dark, silent grave is looked upon as containing life immortal springing into being, and the sepulcher but a chamber of repose.

TIME.

Sed fugit, interea, fugit irreparabile tempus. — VIRG., *Georg. III, 284.*

'Tis a mistake : time flies not,
  He only hovers on the wing :
Once born, the moment dies not,
  'Tis an immortal thing ;
While all is change beneath the sky,
Fix'd like the sun, as learned sages prove,
Though from our moving world he seems to move,
'Tis time stands still, and we that fly.

There is no past ; from nature's birth,
  Days, months, years, ages, till the end
Of these revolving heavens and earth,
  All to one centre tend ;
And, having reach'd it late or soon,
  Converge,—as in a lens, the rays,
Caught from the fountain-light of noon,
  Blend in a point that blinds the gaze :
— What has been is, what is shall last ;
The present is the *focus* of the past ;
The future, perishing as it arrives,
Becomes the present, and itself survives.

Time is not *progress*, but *amount* ;
  One vast accumulating store,
Laid up, not lost ;—we do not count
  Years *gone*, but *added* to the score
Of wealth untold, to clime nor class confined,
Riches to generations lent,
For ever spending, never spent,
Th' august inheritance of all mankind.
Of this, from Adam to his latest heir,
All in due turn their portion share,
Which, as they husband or abuse,
Their souls they win or lose.

                   —MONTGOMERY.

PROPERTY OWNED BY THE CEMETERY COMPANY.

The following report from the Superintendent gives a complete detailed description of the property owned by the Cemetery Company, with its present and pospective uses, which will be interesting to compare with the map of the ground that was also prepared by him:

I. D. G. NELSON, Esq., *President of Lindenwood Cemetery:*

SIR—In compliance with your request, making sundry inquiries, I herewith submit the following:

No. of sections laid out in lots, exclusive of Hebrew section.

Sections H, B, D, F, G, J, R, S, and part of U.

No. of lots in all, 1,303.

No. of lots and subdivisions sold, 1,023.

No. of lots and subdivisions unsold, 259.

Total area covered by lots in all sections, $18\frac{43}{100}$ acres.

Amount of ground occupied by single graves in potter's field, Sections F and S, $1\frac{69}{100}$ acres.

Amount of ground occupied by single graves, other than potter's field, 3,180 square feet.

Area in avenues, $7\frac{89}{100}$ acres.

Length of avenues, 4 miles and 180 feet.

Area of back lot, $26\frac{1}{2}$ acres.

Low ground, unfit for interment purposes, about 25 acres, but well adapted to lawn and meadow purposes, for which it is used.

Amount of ground remaining available for interments, 70 acres.

Total area of Cemetery at present time, 124 acres.

Very Respectfully,

DECEMBER 31, 1885.   JOHN H. DOSWELL, *Supt.*

CARE OF LOTS.

We have heretofore called the attention of lot owners to this subject, and now repeat it, that to secure a general good effect in the cemetery it is essential that every lot should be well cared for, as a single neglected lot, overgrown with tall grass and weeds, mars the beauty of a whole section. It is a duty which every lot owner owes to the Cemetery Company, to every other lot owner, and to himself and his family, to preserve from neglect the home of his dead.

The work of mowing all the grounds, including the lots, two or three

times during the summer and gather the fallen leaves, limbs and other rubbish, is a large item of expense that has heretofore been mainly borne by the Company—a generous custom not practiced by most other cemeteries. In the commencement, when the improved grounds were small and other portions exposed to view were in an unsightly condition, and for the purpose of preserving as much harmony of appearance as possible, it was thought advisable to dress the lots that were sold, as well as the rest of the ground. This has doubtless added much to the reputation of Lindenwood as being one of the finest, best kept, and most attractive new cemeteries in the country. Lot holders, however, must bear in mind that the grounds are now quite large, and are growing larger, and the expense of taking care of them very great, so that if any extra mowing or other work is asked by lot owners that is not given in course of the regular mowing and cleaning, an extra charge will be made, at the bare cost of the work, by arrangement with the Superintendent.

As the season of the year is approaching when lot owners' attention is very naturally drawn to their burial lots, and especially those whose dearest and sweetest treasures are deposited there are moved with a desire to add some further token of love and regard ; the first, if not the chief thought is to plant something that will grow and flourish over the graves of dear ones. However satisfactory such planting may be for a time, it not unfrequently is found in a few years to become unsightly, and mar, if not wholly destroy, the natural beauty of the rich, green, soft, velvety grass that the sun loves to shine upon, and which we all so much admire.

At a meeting of the Trustees, held February 14, 1884, the following proceedings were had, and the order published and posted on the grounds with such good results that we append the same as being worthy to be kept in constant remembrance :

NOTICE TO LOT OWNERS AND OTHERS.

WHEREAS, In addition to providing a suitable place for the burial of our dead in Lindenwood Cemetery, it was also a leading feature of the original incorporators, that it should be made a cheerful and pleasant place for the living as well- which feature the Trustees have aimed to keep in view, and still wish to see observed. Accordingly they have witnessed with regret the disastrous effects the cold of the past few winters has had upon certain evergreens and other trees and plants on the grounds, and especially the arbor vitæ hedges enclosing burial lots, giving them a ragged and unsightly appearance. Therefore, it is hereby

Ordered, That no further planting of the same be permitted, except to repair breaches in hedges heretofore planted, and even then, in most cases, their entire removal would add greatly to the appearance of the lot, if only covered with a well-kept blue grass sward. It is also further

Ordered, That the planting of Irish juniper and other tender trees and plants by owners of lots be discouraged in all cases, and where trees, plants or shrubbery of any kind have died, the Superintendent is required to remove the same and charge the cost of such removal to the owners of the lots, as other expenses and improvements are charged and collected.

And it is suggested as being in the line of economy and good taste, that, before giving orders for ornamental trees and shrubbery, it would be well for lot holders to consult the Superintendent in regard to how little, instead of how much, money should be expended in improvements best suited to the purpose; for the truth is, that only few very choice, strictly ornamental trees are in harmony with good taste, when applied to our own beautiful burial grounds. Nature has supplied us with her choicest treasures to make the scenery of Lindenwood both appropriate and attractive.

COMMON ENEMY OF CEMETERIES.

"The mole that scoops with curious toil
Her subterranean bed,
Thinks not she ploughs a human soil,
And mines among the dead."

One of the greatest pests the Superintendent of Lindenwood has had to contend with has been the ground mole, a threatened destroyer of the cemetery's special charms. A few years ago the whole ground seemed becoming alive with them, rooting and loosening up the sod wherever it seemed the most thrifty and healthiest, which threatened, if not the total destruction, to seriously mar the chief beauty of our fine blue grass sward, the attractive feature of all handsomely kept lawns, parks or cemetery grounds. From the ready adaptation and free growth of this species of grass it was expected to make it, at least, one of the leading features of beauty, so highly prized by all cemetery managers.

The destructive work of these little animals went on from bad to worse, rooting up and honeycombing the whole ground wherever grass was growing the most luxuriantly, well nigh discouraging Superintendent Doswell, who tried many recommended schemes of destruction without any satisfactory results. He at last saw a newspaper description of two different kinds of "mole traps" that looked like meeting the necessities of the case. He ordered samples of each, the "Isbell" and the "Hale." They both proved to be what was needed, and for the past two years have caught large quantities of these precious little rascals. The disastrous work of these moles is not confined to cemeteries, parks or lawns, but the products of thousands of acres of pasture and meadow land is now annually destroyed in this section of country alone by the depredations of these little voracious, subterranean creatures, who are always "as fat as a mole." And the time is not distant when farmers, as well as others, will be compelled to hunt them more vigorously than all other pests that annoy them. These depredators' home and food are both in the earth. She does no foraging, nor is she ever seen above the surface, of her own volition; but, on the contrary, is very sensitive to the presence of a tread over or near her, and her movements of retreat are too expert for any dog, and her suspicions apparently too intelligent to take poison, so that on every account she is a troublesome customer to deal with.

FUNERAL EXTRAVAGANCE.

Its career has been checked in England, where it has been most profligate and where reform has been most needed, but least expected. The spirit of extravagance has been creeping into American society at a shocking rate, until at last a halt has been called. Of late, funerals in large cities, among what is considered the wealthy and aristocratic families, have in many instances been of the plainest and least expensive character. The example is a praiseworthy one.

Of the reform in England the *London Daily News* speaks of the third annual meeting of the society called the "Church of England Funeral and Mourning Association," which aims to promote the following results: First, to encourage the adoption of such observances only as are consistent with a hope of resurrection to eternal life; second, to discourage feasting on the day of burial, and all useless or extravagant expenditure in the coffin and its furniture on the occasion of the funeral, and in the wearing of mourning. The Society adopts the broad ground that the funerals should be conducted and mourning worn without the unmeaning pomp, vain ostentation and dismal pageantry of hat-bands, scarfs, plumes, mourning coaches, heavy crape trimmings, and the like, which are quite inconsistent with a hopeful belief in a future state, involve unprofitable expenditure, inflict severe hardship upon persons of limited means, and neither mitigate grief nor manifest respect for the dead. It offers as suggestions: That every part of the solemn rite of burial be made a labor of love, to the exclusion, as far as possible, of paid labor; that the body be buried in a plain wood coffin in the earth itself, with nothing to arrest its return to earth whence it was taken; that perhaps the best plan that has been suggested, that both men and women wear a band of black cloth on the arm to indicate that a death has taken place in the family; and that all headstones and memorials be Christian in character. It is stated that Peers (the Archbishop of York, the Marquises of Abergavenny, Aylesbury and Ripon, Earl Fitzwilliam, nearly all the bishops and many others), members of Parliament, officers in the army and navy, clergymen, physicians, lawyers and merchants have given their adhesion to the general principle of funeral and mourning reform, including the Mayor of Leicester, the Archdeacon of Leicester, Alderman Stafford, most of the clergy of Leicester, and others connected with the town.

Monuments.

While collecting materials for this work, it was suggested as being appropriate and in harmony with good taste to distribute a few cuts of the monuments erected on the grounds among the pages of this work—a suggestion that only required to be mentioned to obtain as many as space would permit to be inserted, from the generous owners, without expense to the corporation. They were handsomely lithographed by Mr. Wm. B. Burford, of Indianapolis, from accurate photographs, taken by Mr. John A. Shoaf, of Fort Wayne. They give a very fair representation of the whole, of which Lindenwood is as handsomely and as appropriately furnished as any cemetery of which we have any knowledge. Our people appreciate the propriety of the erection of monuments and substantial head-stones in proportion to their ability to do so. And there is also a generous liberality in the erection of costly ones by those who can afford it; for, while it has special reference and interest in marking the place of burial of family remains, it is also of general interest to every lot-owner, whatever his circumstances or condition in life. Every lot-holder has an equitable interest in the whole grounds, in proportion to the amount invested, and consequently should, and doubtless does, take a laudable pride in whatever adds to the ornamentation and beauty of the whole grounds. We have occasionally heard it remarked, that it was a great waste of money to erect expensive monuments. It must not be so regarded. It is, on the contrary, a charitable use of the money; for, aside of its eminent fitness in commemoration of departed relatives and friends, it is in the line and interest of unselfish labor. For, if a monument is erected at a cost, say of $20,000, at least $19,975 will be paid out for labor in one form and another that might otherwise lie idle, doing no good to any person or community. The endless quantities of granite and marble that abound in this and in other parts of the globe, are worth comparatively but a trifle in their native quarry beds, and, therefore, the monument is almost purely the product of labor from the time the first stroke of the quarryman's drill is heard until the skilled mechanic wipes off his trowel on his apron at the tomb and pronounces his work finished.

Lithographed views of the following monuments will be found distributed through the pages of this work, in the order in which they were erected:

Before furnishing a list of the monuments here mentioned, we would state that there have been, including 403 removals from other cemeteries, a total of 4,926 interments to date.

The Bass monument, on section "II," was erected in 1863, to the memory of Col. Sion S. Bass, who fell at Shiloh, by his regiment and friends. It is an appropriate marble shaft eighteen feet high, draped with the American flag—a fitting tribute to his bravery and patriotism.

The Hanna monument, erected in 1864, on section "B," by the heirs of Judge Samuel Hanna, is of Italian marble, die style, twelve feet high, appropriately ornamented with trusses. In workmanship and finish, equaled by few of its class.

The Ewing monument, on section "B," erected in 1870, is a Scotch, highly-polished, granite obelisk, thirty-five feet high, resting on a Quincy granite base eight feet square. It is said to be the largest and finest single shaft of Scotch granite in America. It was selected and erected by Mr. B. D. Miner, executor of the estate of Col. George W. Ewing.

The Edgerton monument is an obelisk of Italian marble, twenty feet high, sound and beautiful when erected in 1872, on section "J," but is now disintegrating and showing signs of decay. Mr. Alfred P. Edgerton, by whom it was erected, has provided for its restoration, if ever needed, by a wise and liberal provision to the bequest fund, which was made before any signs of decay began to appear.

The Williams monument was erected by Mr. Jesse L. Williams, on section "G," in 1875. It is an obelisk of Westerly, Rhode Island, granite, twenty-eight feet high, hammer-dressed, of massive, fine and commanding proportions.

The Simons monument is of Westerly, Rhode Island, granite, erected in 1876 by Mr. Oscar A. Simons. It is of cottage style, hammer-dressed, with polished die, twelve feet high; one of the most attractive and solid works of the kind on section "D."

The Wood monument, a sarcophagus, from the Hallowell, Me., quarries; lower base, eleven feet six inches by eight feet six inches; height, nine feet. It was exhibited at the Centennial, at Philadelphia, in 1876, and erected on section "J," same year. The workmanship is surpassingly fine, and the style attractive. It was erected by Mrs. George W. Wood in memory of her husband.

The Morgan monument, on section "II," was erected in 1884 by Mr. Oliver P. Morgan. It is made of Quincy (Mass.) granite, cottage style, ornamented with columns and capitals; height, ten feet; hammer-dressed, with polished die; distinct and attractive.

THE BEQUEST FUND.

This is a subject which is now everywhere attracting the attention of cemetery companies.

The trustees of Greenwood Cemetery, New York, make these remarks on this important subject: "We can hardly imagine that the feeling which has prompted a costly purchase and erection should be unaccompanied with a desire that a spot, on which so much has been spent, should always be kept in neatness and good repair. To the very natural wish that one's own place of final repose should ever be decent and respectable, a still stronger motive is added by our regard for the memory of others. But these lots and monuments will not take care of themselves. No pains or expense in the outset—no solidity of material—no thoroughness of workmanship—is proof against the perpetual tendencies to deformity and decay. In cases of this sort, the action of nature may prove unfriendly alike in processes of growth and of decomposition. Trees, shrubs, briars and weeds soon fill a neglected lot with their tangled and squalid growth. Headstones and monuments are seldom placed so firmly as to defy forever the powerful forces which are constantly at work to weaken and throw them down. We believe that many, who have provided in Greenwood a last resting-place for themselves and their kindred, would gladly insure their grounds and improvements against such effacing and destroying influences. They know that they can not be always on the spot to watch the beginning and progress of decay, and do not forget that their own personal care can, at the best, continue but a litttle while. It is still less to be expected that those who may come after them should do what they, themselves, have failed to accomplish."

It is only necessary to refer to our own old Fort Wayne Cemetery for confirmation of all that has been or can be said on this subject.

LINDENWOOD BEQUEST.

One of the leading objects of this organization being the placing it upon a foundation of securing forever its being kept up in good condition, and as a guide to those who may wish to bequeath to the Cemetery for specific or general purposes, we insert the following form, which, in substance, is used in other cemeteries. Doubtless many of our citizens will gladly avail themselves of an opportunity to give to Lindenwood Cemetery, where lie many dear friends, and where they hope to lie down themselves, a sum sufficient to render much good to those who follow them and secure forever the care and attention necessary to the protection and improvement of their own grounds. What tender associations, what kind memories, what inspiring thoughts, what Christian hopes will be awakened in the breasts of those for whose benefit it will be conferred :

FORM OF BEQUEST FOR BENEFIT OF IMPROVEMENTS.

. . . ., of the city of . . . . county of . . . ., State of . . . ., being the owner of lot No . . . ., in Section . . . ., of "The Lindenwood Cemetery," desiring to maintain and keep said lot and all monuments, improvements and appurtenances thereon in perfect condition and preservation, as far as is practicable, do hereby give and pay to "The Lindenwood Cemetery" aforesaid the sum of . . . . dollars.

To have and to hold the same to the said Lindenwood Cemetery and its successors forever, in trust, however, to keep the same securely invested at a rate of interest of not less than six per cent. per annum, payable annually ; and to apply from year to year the interest arising from such sum thus invested, or as much of it as may be necessary to carry out the provisions of this deed, under the direction of the Board of Trustees of said Lindenwood Cemetery, to the repair and preservation of any tomb, monument or gravestone erected, or to be erected, on said lot, and such other improvements as may be deemed proper and in harmony with good taste, and in general keeping of the whole grounds.

PROVIDED, HOWEVER, The said Trustees shall not be responsible for their conduct in the discharge of said trust, except for good faith and such reasonable diligence as may be required of mere gratuitous agents.

In testimony whereof, the said . . . . ha . affixed . . . hand and seal, and the said Lindenwood Cemetery does hereby acknowledge by the signature of its President and its seal hereto affixed, the receipt of said sum of . . . . dollars paid to its Treasurer, and does accept the trust by this instrument.

Signed and sealed this . . . day of . . . . . ., 18 .

As an evidence of the importance attached to this feature of Cemetery organization among thoughtful people, we notice that the lot owners of Greenwood Cemetery, of Brooklyn, N. Y., which is but eight years older than Lindenwood, have already deposited with the corporation $154,897.41 to insure future care and protection until time shall be no more.

The Hon. Alfred P. Edgerton, the heirs of Hon. Pliny Hoagland and Jared D. Bond, Esq., have deposited to the credit of the Lindenwood bequest fund a liberal sum each, for the future care and protection of their lots and monuments. Others are preparing to do the same.

IN CONCLUSION— I will remark that, in compliance with the request of the Board, I herewith submit a detailed report of the transactions of this Association from the date of its organization to the present time. In this I have been materially aided by the Secretary, Treasurer and Superintendent, in furnishing from time to time such information in their several departments as I have needed to make the work as complete as possible to an intelligent understanding of the lot owners, as well as others who may take an interest in our beautiful city of the dead—the sepulchral home prepared by the living. All matters thought to be of sufficient interest to be inserted will be found under different heads in appropriate places. It is true we have no rugged hills or towering mountains, no cascades or startling water-falls, or vast expanse of ocean scenery to attract romantic admiration, some, or all of which, others may have. But we must be content with what we have as being less to be admired perhaps by those in search of romance, but such as is far more appropriate and beautiful to those whose hearts and affections are centered here in Lindenwood. While reflecting upon the fact that nature furnished to our hands a most wonderful preparation of virgin soil that had never been disturbed by man, already moulded in shape and form as no human hands could equal, with crowned hills and gentle elevations, beautiful plateaus, glades, glens and water-courses, miles of well-defined avenues for drives as well as for cemetery uses (just enough and not too many), shaded on either side and to hill-tops by its own native forest trees, whose emerald foliage are in harmonious contrast with the soft, green carpet of grass on either side, and the azure hues of the skies above. No such apparent miraculous instance of Divine workmanship as is here presented in furnishing a perfect foundation for a silent city has anywhere else been observed. Not a hill has been cut down, or the location of an avenue materially changed, but everything remains substantially as it came from the hands of its Maker. This has enabled our Landscape Architect and Superintendent, Mr. Doswell, an opportunity to develop his taste, skill and ingenuity in the general improvement of the whole grounds, which has, I take pleasure in saying, been well done and to the satisfaction of the Board, and the marked admiration of all visitors.

I. D. G. NELSON,

JANUARY 1, 1886.   *President.*

Since the body of this report was printed, an arrangement was consummated with Mr. McCulloch, and the following deed, duly executed, was transmitted to the City Council, and with all of its conditions unanimously accepted by said Council, on the 23d day of February, 1886, an act highly creditable to all parties concerned:

DEED OF "THE McCULLOCH PARK."

WHEREAS, Hugh McCulloch, in the year 1839, purchased of Samuel Hanna the hereinafter described land for a cemetery, which has been known as the Broadway Cemetery, and which was then near Fort Wayne, in Allen county, and State of Indiana, and is now within the limits of the city: and

WHEREAS, The lots into which said land was divided were, from time to time, sold by said McCulloch for burial purposes only; and

WHEREAS, Said cemetery has not been used for such purpose and the remains of the larger part of those who were buried there have been removed, and as a consequence it has been neglected and become unsightly; and

WHEREAS, The said city of Fort Wayne is desirous of obtaining a title to the land in order that it may be converted into a park, to be called the "McCulloch Park," and permanently held and improved as such; now

Hugh McCulloch, and Susan McCulloch, the wife of said Hugh, now of Prince George's county, and State of Maryland, in consideration of the premises and of one dollar, to us paid by said city of Fort Wayne, the receipt of which is hereby acknowledged, and of the conditions hereinafter named, do hereby assign, convey, and quit claim to said city and its successors, all our right and title to and interest in said cemetery, and to the land upon which it was laid off, and which land is described as follows:

Four acres, more or less, in the west half of the northwest quarter of section eleven (11), township thirty (30) north of range twelve (12) east. Beginning at a stone at the northwest corner of said four acres, thence south 81½ degrees, west thirty-two (32) rods, thence south 58¾ degrees, west twenty (20) rods, thence north 31½ degrees, east thirty-two rods, thence north 58¾ degrees, east twenty rods to the place of beginning, a plat of which four acres is on record in the recorder's office, Allen county, in book C, page 410, with a diagram of the ground.

This conveyance is, however, on these conditions, to-wit: That the said city shall, within one year, enclose the land by a proper fence and commence the improvement of the same for a park, and continue to improve it in a tasteful and becoming manner, and forever preserve and maintain it as a public park under the name of "The McCulloch Park;" and the said city receives this conveyance upon the express condition that whenever said city or its successors shall fail to preserve and maintain it as a public park, this conveyance shall be void.

In witness whereof we have hereunto set our hands and affixed our seals this 5th day of February, 1886.

HUGH McCULLOCH, {SEAL}

SUSAN McCULLOCH, {SEAL}

LINDENWOOD CEMETERY LOTS.

SECTION B.

SECTION U.

TREASURER'S REPORT.

STATEMENT OF RECEIPTS.

YEARS.	1859	1860	1861	1862	1863	1864	1865
Balance		$379 11				$500 38	$869 67
Cash advanced by Corporators	$2950 00	350 00					65 50
Cash received from sale of burial lots		2489 08	$388 33	$476 40	$3067 80	3068 00	1237 85
Cash received for interments, improvements, etc		58 50	270 65	207 92	396 43	586 10	637 00
Cash received from bills payable		1000 00					
Cash received from bills receivable		500 00	103 50	703 00	664 20	585 50	734 00
Cash received from interest			6 51	19 42	31 79	26 60	75 92
Balance		15 47	115 17	86 81			37 58
Total	$2950 00	$4792 08	$884 16	$1493 55	$4160 22	$4766 58	$3657 52

STATEMENT OF EXPENDITURES.

YEARS.	1859	1860	1861	1862	1863	1864	1865
Balance			$15 47	$115 17	$86 81		
Cash paid for real estate	$1906 87					$530 00	
Cash paid for engineering, clearing, etc	579 12	$648 96					
Cash paid for labor, tools, etc	35 00	688 02	230 64	272 63	712 63	1115 00	$1922 02
Cash paid for salaries of officers		362 00	350 00	420 40	559 60	640 00	1692 50
Cash paid for improvements	49 90	715 00	41 65	241 44	232 30	65 53	43 00
Cash paid for bills payable		1906 87		425 00	1700 00	813 75	
Cash paid for interest		451 23	233 40	8 91	108 00	682 63	
Cash refunded corporators		20 00	13 00	10 00	260 50	50 00	
Balance on hand	379 11					500 38	869 67
Total	$2950 00	$4792 08	$884 16	$1493 55	$4160 22	$4766 58	$3657 52

STATEMENT OF RECEIPTS.

YEARS.	1866	1867	1868	1869	1870	1871	1872
Balance		$563 62			$1 29	$383 04	$1072 88
Cash advanced by corporators							
Cash received from sale of burial lots	$994 40	489 25	$1967 13	$1600 00	2766 16	2393 50	3377 25
Cash received for interments, improvements, etc	791 39	663 78	720 63	808 25	596 00	724 40	1070 50
Cash received from sale of city bonds					1150 00		
Cash received from bills receivable	942 50	192 50	419 00	816 50	1205 00	919 11	1071 07
Cash received from interest	56 25	11 72	21 75	71 00	164 85	175 47	180 15
Balance			88 76	249 50			
Total	$2781 54	$2009 63	$3387 01	$3295 75	$5883 30	$4595 52	$6772 15

STATEMENT OF EXPENDITURES.

YEARS.	1866	1867	1868	1869	1870	1871	1872
Balance	$37 58	....	$88 76	$249 50	..	..	..
Cash paid for real estate							
Cash paid for engineering, clearing, etc.							
Cash paid for labor, tools, etc.	1253 40	$1115 98	1105 38	1089 46	$1312 75	$1495 49	$1621 29
Cash paid for salaries of officers	910 00	890 00	1040 00	890 00	1045 00	1170 00	1120 00
Cash paid for improvements	16 94	3 65	73 62		1031 50	579 15	372 70
Cash paid for bills payable				200 00	950 00	200 00	2345 12
Cash paid on acct. of bills receivable							333 34
Cash paid for interest				63 00	361 73	78 00	858 18
Cash refunded to corporators			79 25				
Cash paid for city and county orders			1000 00				
Cash paid for attorney's fees				802 50	799 28		
Balance on hand	563 62			1 29	383 04	1072 88	121 52
Total	$2781 54	$2009 63	$3387 01	$3295 75	$5883 30	$4595 52	$6772 15

STATEMENT OF RECEIPTS.

YEARS.	1873	1874	1875	1876	1877	1878	1879
Balance	$121 52	$1194 99	$2444 08	$52 67	$15 15	$413 51	$352 00
Cash advanced by corporators							
Cash received from sale of burial lots	1720 75	2800 00	2897 50	1116 25	1480 00	1015 00	1865 00
Cash received for interments, improvements, etc.	843 65	925 74	920 85	807 25	774 25	819 60	866 00
Cash received from sale of wood, hay, etc.			114 10	244 75	955 11	109 50	75 87
Cash received from bills receivable	2896 17	1991 42	1819 50	1349 25	1436 25	1143 00	492 00
Cash received from interest	240 37	230 55	264 00	107 82	174 60	141 00	55 10
Cash received on acct. of bequests	560 00						
Balance							
Total	$6382 46	$7142 70	$8460 03	$3677 99	$4835 39	$3641 61	$3706 27

STATEMENT OF EXPENDITURES.

YEARS.	1873	1874	1875	1876	1877	1878	1879
Balance							
Cash paid for real estate							
Cash paid for engineering, clearing, etc.							
Cash paid for labor, tools, etc.	$1805 87	$2132 49	$2140 54	$2002 74	$1453 12	$1402 29	$1211 60
Cash paid for salaries of officers	1410 00	1340 00	1660 00	1510 00	1190 00	1260 00	1380 00
Cash paid for improvements			1225 63	1122 37	150 10		128 16
Cash paid for bills payable	1667 00		2253 90		1521 00	473 20	600 00
Cash paid on acct. of bills receivable			95 00				
Cash paid for interest	304 60	50	19 40		257 76	154 12	
Cash paid for repairs to road to Cemetery			1116 15				
Balance on hand	1194 99	2444 08	52 67	15 15	413 51	352 00	386 42
Total	$6382 46	$7142 70	$8460 03	$3677 99	$4835 39	$3641 61	$3706 27

STATEMENT OF RECEIPTS.

YEARS.	1880	1881	1882	1883	1884	1885
Balance	$396 42	$16 45	$2784 13	$6898 23	$5169 30	$2673 24
Cash received from sale of burial lots	1952 50	3312 50	2291 40	1937 50	2310 50	1650 00
Cash received from interments, improvements, etc	846 50	1184 50	1120 50	970 75	1056 50	988 00
Cash received from sale of wood, hay, etc	18 70	259 25	21 50	94 40	51 50	35 00
Cash received from bills receivable	2203 32	786 61	3607 00	553 50	6135 00	414 50
Cash received from interest	179 75	184 89	198 54	89 22	350 27	27 70
Cash received on account of bequests						525 00
Cash received on account of A. P. Edgerton, improvement account		150 00			60 00	
Total	$5687 19	$5894 20	10023 07	10543 60	15133 07	$6313 44

STATEMENT OF EXPENDITURES.

YEARS.	1880	1881	1882	1883	1884	1885
Balance						
Cash paid for real estate						
Cash paid for engineering, clearing, etc.						
Cash paid for labor, tools, etc	$1347 37	$1558 34	$1659 44	$1598 80	$2658 10	$1591 96
Cash paid for salaries of officers	1280 00	1300 00	1350 00	1250 00	1280 00	1320 00
Cash paid for improvements	36 87	95 64	115 40	43 50	8161 73	1403 68
Cash paid for bills payable	1668 80					
Cash paid on account bills receivable				12 00		
Cash paid for interest	1257 70	156 09			60 00	
Cash paid for money loaned				2500 00		
Balance on hand	16 45	2784 13	6898 23	5169 30	2673 24	1997 80
Total	$5587 19	$5894 20	10023 07	10543 60	15133 07	$6313 44

TRIAL BALANCE, DECEMBER 31, 1885.

Improvement account		Lindenwood Cemetery	5935 34
Old National Bank	$1997 80	In Trust and Bequest account	1000 00
Bills receivable	1964 75	A. P. Edgerton improvement acct	24 50
J. H. Doswell		J. H. Doswell	240 00
Building account	6864 79		
Estate P. Hoagland, improvement account	13 50		
Protection account	250 00		
Total	$11190 84	Total	$11190 84

www.ingramcontent.com/pod-product-compliance
Lightning Source LLC
Chambersburg PA
CBHW021533270326
41930CB00008B/1225